THROW THE DAMN BALL

THROW THE DAMN BALL

CLASSIC POETRY BY DOGS

R. D. ROSEN, HARRY PRICHETT, AND ROB BATTLES

A PLUME BOOK

PLUME
Published by the Penguin Group
Penguin Group (USA) LLC
375 Hudson Street
New York, New York 10014

USA | Canada | UK | Ireland | Australia | New Zealand | India | South Africa | China
penguin.com
A Penguin Random House Company

First published by Plume, a member of Penguin Group (USA) LLC, 2013

 REGISTERED TRADEMARK—MARCA REGISTRADA

CIP data is available.
ISBN 978-0-14-218085-3

Printed in the United States of America
10 9 8 7 6

Set in Neutraface
Designed by Daniel Lagin

CONTENTS

INTRODUCTION

The pleasure of discovering these poems has been indescribable. To glimpse the scope and depths of these animals' most private feelings, and their astonishing ability to express them, forces all of us to revise upward our already high opinion of these devoted creatures.

More remarkable still, these dogs reveal more than a passing acquaintance with Western human poetry, as evidenced by the many verses in this volume alluding to great works by Robert Frost, Emily Dickinson, Dylan Thomas, William Butler Yeats, William Carlos Williams, John Donne, Allen Ginsberg, Joyce Kilmer, Helen Reddy, and others. These canine bards have used the immortal lines of others to head off in unexpected directions, not unlike a dog let off a short leash in a city park.

Perhaps it's the dog's wolf ancestry that explains the wildness and earthiness of some of these verses. While most of the poems in this volume reflect classic themes—like love, loss, friendship, and mealtime—there is also an emphasis on sex and bodily functions, the lack of which in human poetry may well explain its decline in popularity. We've made no attempt to censor these works, subscribing, as we do, to the "Write what you know" edict familiar to writers of all species. These poems challenge us not to hold our noses at the mention of poop, pee, and flatulence, and to explore their deeper meanings.

Be open-minded. Embrace these dogs' efforts to be better understood. In so doing, we may come to know ourselves better, and the dogs within all of us.

—The Editors

NO!

When you say NO!
There is no love behind your jabbing,
*   pointed finger.*

When you say NO!
There is no tenderness in your scary,
*   rigid body.*

When you say NO!
There is no joy in your angry,
*   contorted face.*

When you say NO!
I feel I must cower, then slink away to
*   soil your favorite things.*

You should learn another word.

GRACIE

BRONX, NEW YORK

I AM DOG,
HEAR MY GROWLS

I am dog, hear my growls.
Something's happening in my bowels.
I hope you have some paper towels.

BANJO
BRONX, NEW YORK

TO MY SHORT-LEGGED MISTRESS

My nerves circle inside me like a hungry hawk
While waiting for the clatter of your nails up the walk.
My head tells me it should be no big deal,
But my heart can't wait till I hear you squeal.
While the rest of dogdom makes do with the dregs,
We'll be making the beast with eight legs.

WILLY
COOLIDGE, GEORGIA

FLOAT LIKE A MALAMUTE

Float like a malamute
Sting like a saluki
I look kind of cute
But when I hit you, you'll puki

SCHUYLER
SOUTH BURLINGTON, VERMONT

HEY, GOOD-LOOKIN'

Sure, I'm a floozy.
Drink makes me woozy.
But you look too boozy
Yourself to be choosy.

WINGER
CARMEL, INDIANA

I HOPE YOU'RE HAVING FUN

Your lack of kindness—it shows.
Your imagination? Not fecund.
You're not the owner I would have chose;
My hate for you deepens and grows
With every single second
This biscuit stays on my nose.

COPPER
SANTA CRUZ, CALIFORNIA

O BEAUTIFUL
ABSORBENT LAND

O beautiful absorbent land,
Too vast to find itself defiled
By any single dog or child!
So spacious it's as if you planned
That every mountain, plain,
*   and river,*
Every sacred rock and stump
Beseeched my very bowels
*   to quiver!*
On you I proudly take a dump.

ARCHIE
LEVITTOWN, PENNSYLVANIA

DO NOT GO GENTLE

Do not go gentle into that dog run,
For a dog my size, it isn't fun.
When they see me, big dogs go mental.
Into that dog run I shall not go gentle.

KINA
NEW PALTZ, NEW YORK

NEUTERED

Flames of desire snuffed.
Trembling hindquarters stilled.
Moans of passion silenced.

BUSTER
PITTSTON, PENNSYLVANIA

STARTLED BY A BIRD

A flutter.
A bird in the bush.
A wrinkle of wind.
The shadow of flight.

I couldn't care less.

MARBURY
STAMFORD, CONNECTICUT

ISLAND

No dog is an island.
Every dog's death diminishes me.
Except perhaps for Stanley,
The Hoffendahls' mean Akita.
I'm better off with him dead.

JET
NASHVILLE, TENNESSEE

FOR YOUR LOVE

For your love I've always yearned.
In the past, though, I've been burned.
Can you blame me for looking so concerned?

HATHOS
LAUSANNE, SWITZERLAND

HOME SWEET HOMEY

I'm a round mound of bad hound
Sprung from the bowels of the city
    pound,
A damp, dirty dog underground—
A pit full of bull and yappin' mutts,
The whinin' Lab and the poodle who
    struts,
Bichon who bays and the King
    Charles who tuts.
Let me tell you, I survived by growl
    and guile
Until you gave me a reason to smile
By furnishing me with a domicile.
Word.

FIFTY SCENT
WASHINGTON HEIGHTS, NEW YORK

SONG OF THE SKUNK CABBAGE

By the shores of Gitche Gumee,
By the shining Falling-Water,
Sat a sated son of nature,
Breaking wind with sacred pleasure.

MR. TUPELO HONEY WOLFF
NORTHAMPTON, MASSACHUSETTS

WHAT I LOOK FOR IN A POEM

What I look for in a poem is grace,
In which each word knows its place
And metaphors flow out of sense,
And there's consistency of tense.

I look for poems about rabies
Or the threat posed by dogs to
    babies,
That focus on scabies or skin
    conditions
Or dogs who can't control their
    emissions.

But all of it done in extremely
    good taste!
Because a poem is a horrible thing
    to waste.

SIR KNIGHTON JACKSON
ASHLAND, MASSACHUSETTS

JUST ONE MORE TREAT

Just one more treat
I won't ask again
Just one more treat
And I'll go to my den

Just one more treat
It's just a suggestion
Just one more treat
It's good for digestion

Just one more treat
Perhaps a small bone
Just one more treat
And I'll leave you alone

LUNA
HELLERTOWN, PENNSYLVANIA

WHOSE BALL THIS
IS I THINK I KNOW

Whose ball this is I think I know.
I make him throw and throw and throw.
Some will, no doubt, think him a fool
To play the role of dog-whipped wretch
And expose himself to so much drool
As he makes me fetch and fetch and
   fetch.

SPROCKET
KIRKWOOD, NEW YORK

SCRATCH ME ARSE

You'd fancy a jaunt through the park, I'm sure.
Perhaps a spot of tea.
Bloody hell.
I'd rather you just scratch me arse.

BRUTUS
CORAL SPRINGS, FLORIDA

THE CONE SETS A TONE ALL ITS OWN

Please don't tell me that I'm all alone
In loving the fashion effect of the cone.
I'm aware it's considered completely
*   heretical*
To wear it for reasons strictly unmedical,
But I like the way it frames my face
And gives my head its very own space.

I've been told it makes me look rather
*   regal*
(Anyway, that's according to
*   McCallister's beagle).*
The only downside, if I may be crass,
Is that it makes it impossible to sniff
*   my own ass.*

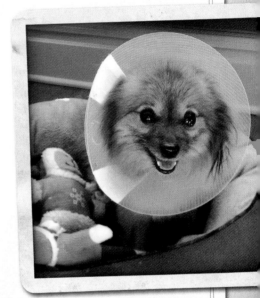

RACER
MAPLEWOOD, NEW JERSEY

LIFT MY SKIRT

Lift my skirt, but say you love me
Under the stands with the crowd above me.
Watch out for the pom-poms, don't touch my ear
And only make noise when the crowd starts to cheer.

Two, four, eleven, nine,
I can't count, but I sure am fine.

GRAVY
BABYLON, NEW YORK

AWAY

Away from the crowds, strange petters, and bustle,
Away from the kennels and chaos and hustle,
Away from cheap toys of rubber and hide,
I come here to find me and what's inside.

MILLHOUSE
CAMBRIDGE, MASSACHUSETTS

YOU DISGUST ME

look at you
standing there
so superior
barking orders
as if I'd listen
to your high-pitched
*   voice*
and pathetic commands
look at you
you disgust me

SKIPPY
VERONA, NEW JERSEY

JOWL

O, friendly flap of flesh,
Loose facial handle,
To whose pleasures, ever fresh,
No other flab can hold a candle!

I'm crazy 'bout you, jowl,
So wet and soft and slack.
I raise my voice in soggy howl
That jowls I do not lack.

NEKO
WASHINGTON, D.C.

NIMBY

Take your crap elsewhere! Don't be so seedy!
Can't you poop at your own place?
Who said my patch was yours to deface
With your artless fecal graffiti?
C'mon, buddy, and be a trooper
Not an indiscriminate, wandering pooper!
Like me, you wouldn't find it hard
To bark: Hey! Not In My Back Yard.

MESA
SCOTTSDALE, ARIZONA

I SAW YOU ONCE

I saw you once across a snowy field
That beneath a patina of ice had
*   congealed.*
Your glance thawed my heart and
*   my senses reeled.*
I felt as though our fates were sealed.

Your aroma still lingers in the
*   frosty air.*
I've barked your name too many
*   times to count.*
Where did you go? It isn't fair.
You looked like you'd be good to
*   mount.*

CHAD
DURANGO, COLORADO

JUST BECAUSE

Just because I'm your best friend,
What makes you think you're mine?
It's sad how on a mutt you depend
For self-esteem and feeling fine,
When you've alienated all your human friends
And stubbornly refuse to make amends,
Leaving me alone to stomach
*   your pity*
And allow you to pet me
*   when you're feeling shitty.*
I've got far better friends
*   than you, you whiner—*
Beginning with Smokey, the
*   Clarks' Weimaraner.*

WILLIAM
GARDINER, NEW YORK

MY FAVORITE TOY

My precious toy, soaked with saliva and pee.
Here, take it—I dare you—and throw it to me.

GINGER
NEW YORK CITY

27

INTO THE S**T-FILLED NIGHT

I'm ready for my walk.
My boots are laced up tight.
So leash me good and send me out
Into the shit-filled night.

Neither glass nor stones nor phlegm in the street,
Nor any of the crap with which the yard's replete
Will cause my sensitive paws to freak
Or stop this dog from taking a leak.

TACO
MERCED, CALIFORNIA

EXCUSE ME IF I DON'T GET UP

Excuse me if I don't get up,
But you can see I'm no longer a pup.
Keep walking if you're looking for frisky
'Cause I can barely move; it's far too risky.
I'm retired from the world and all its pap.
My job now is going from nap to nap.

And now I splay me down to sleep,
The Lord I pray my soul to keep.

WOOF
NEW YORK CITY

THE SEA

The sea, the sea.
I hate the friggin' sea.

RIPLEY
BROOKLYN, NEW YORK

LICKING MY BALLS ON A SNOWY EVENING

Please don't think me queer
That I can bring to my crotch my face
* so near.*
And no comments when I give my balls
* a shake.*
Don't tell me there's been some big
* mistake,*
Because he, you know, who has to tote 'em
Has the right to lick his scrotum.
So pardon me as I enjoy a small snack
By nibbling on my precious ball sac.

BRANDON
BOONTON, NEW JERSEY

VISTA

From up here I can see
All the places I like to pee.
Thank you.

DUNKIN
WAYLAND, MASSACHUSETTS

AFTERGLOW

I lie here in rapture,
Exhausted by our passion.
How can you sit there,
Eating kibble from your bowl?

ROSEMARY
DURANGO, COLORADO

THIS IS JUST TO SAY

I have eaten
the prosciutto slices
you left on
the table
and which
you were probably
saving
for people
forgive me
they were so delicious
and meaty.

P.S. I left you the ziti.

CASSIDY
LONG BEACH, NEW YORK

34

BLOAT

Dogs seldom make passes
At dogs passing gasses.

FURA
COSTA BRAVA, SPAIN

HEAT

I'm Sparky and come from a long line
  of heroes.
The crackle of fire is music to me.
I poured gas on the doghouse behind
  the Shapiros,
So their miserable schnauzer, Luke,
  had to flee.
Now their property's worthless,
  nothing but zeros—
That once stately colonial's naught but
  debris—
That place over there? Used to be the
  Speros'.
Got arrested for that one, but still
  copped a plea.

SPARKY
GLEN COVE, NEW YORK

WHERE ARE YOU?

Stay, stay, you said, and so I stayed.
I trusted you to soon return.
Such a good girl, you cooed, and played
Me for a fool—to early learn
To doubt, and now to be afraid
And human falseness to discern.

ZOOEY
NEW YORK CITY

ODE TO HOSE

O magical source of delirious spray!
O spewing serpent of joy!
O gushing geyser, wet wild display!
You are, by far, my bestest toy!

ZERO
RIVERDALE, NEW YORK

LICK AND LET LICK

I live to lick.
My tongue is quick.
It's also well hung and pink as a lung.
I don't care if I'm rude when I lick my food—
I'll count to ten and I'll lick it again.

MINNIE
MIDDLETOWN, CONNECTICUT

ALONE

Behind these bars of splintered cedar
My days pass like dry leaves in the wind.
The icy clutches of winter force me inward
To a place I call Alone.

ZOE
NEW YORK CITY

DOG LORD

What you lookin' at, fool? You got something to say?
You're on my turf now, chump—best be runnin' away.
You think you can take me? You makin' an error.
I'm four pounds eight ounces of unholy terror.

JOSÉ
NEW YORK CITY

ODE TO ODES

I positively salivate
Over writing that I consider great.
I'm forever and ever on the prowl
For the perfect procession of consonant and vowel.

Nothing compares to discovering the sonnet
That moves me so much that I want to pee on it.

COSMO
NEW ROCHELLE, NEW YORK

HER

Her matted coat.
Her sultry growl.
Her velvet paws.
Her chestnut-brown eyes.
Her great ass.
That's what I miss about her.

BUDDY
WELLFLEET, MASSACHUSETTS

FLY ME TO
THE MOON

Fly me to the moon.
I can't get away from your kids
    too soon.
When they hug me so tight I can't
    catch my breath.
Someday they're gonna love me
    to death.

If I had a phone to get help then I'd dial it.
Can you blame me for wishing that I were a pilot?
Oh for the thrill that steals up
The very moment that we're wheels up!
At five thousand feet, I'd get a much-needed injection
Of relief from all earthly human affection.

WALLY
NEW YORK CITY

INTERVENTION

I don't think I need to mention
That we're here for an intervention.
God knows how often I've repeated
That I can no longer stand the way that I'm
*   treated.*
Bob, your drinking is way out of hand
And from now on your evening scotches are
*   banned.*
Nancy, stop displacing your anger at Bob
On me, and by the way you dress like a slob.
It's my duty to tell you that when the other
*   dogs visit,*
The shame I feel about you both is exquisite.
If you won't confront your demons, I afraid
*   that's that.*
I'm leaving and you can get a cat.

DUKE
CHICAGO

THERE IS NO FRIGATE
LIKE A PAVEMENT

There is no frigate like
a pavement
To carry me far away.
I sail by smells encrusted
there
To lands where senses play.

To you it may be gray
concrete;
To me it is utopia,
Where smells all meld
and mix and meet—
Olfactory cornucopia!

CONSTANTINO
ATHENS, GREECE

SHAMELESS

I'll do absolutely anything to
    please,
Even pretend I can tickle the keys.
I love to hear folks gently scoff,
"How cute! He thinks he's
    Rachmaninoff!"

For laughs, my lack of stuff I strut,
Not knowing Berlioz from my butt.
Tomorrow, you might find me in
    spandex atop the high beam—
Because nothing's too low for my
    self-esteem.

PANJI
SANTA CRUZ, CALIFORNIA

47

THE MIGHTY MOUND

O mound of turd
Sculpted and brown
There you sit
On hallowed ground

My work has weight
It's stately, steady,
Not spindly
Like some Giacometti

But rains will come
And wash you away
Adieu! Adieu!
My fecal decay

O mound of turd
So dark and brown
There you sat
On hallowed ground

JET
NASHVILLE, TENNESSEE

STEP AWAY

That's far enough,
step away from the duck.
Come any closer
and you're totally . . .
getting way too close to the duck.

DEEB
CHICAGO

UNFAMILIAR FIRE

An unfamiliar fire rages inside me,
Consuming me with desire and doubt.
The beast within bays to be free.
Please, please, please let me out.

AMEE
STONE RIDGE, NEW YORK

FETCH ME ANOTHER

I'm strictly an ale dog, and I like to get tight
So pull me a pint, mate, then fetch me another.
By the end of this night, if I'm not in a fight,
You can watch me proposition some other dog's brother.

BELLA
HOLIDAY, FLORIDA

MOBSTERS

Here they come, the lobsters,
Like a crazy bunch of clattering mobsters.
However, they never give me pause
With their rubber-banded claws
And creepy air of imminent doom.
Don't they know there's a pot
Of boiling water in the room?

ROGER
NEW YORK CITY

OUR NOSES GET MORE ERECT

Our noses get more erect
With each new smell that we detect.
It's thrilling, this distilling
Of complex odors while we're chilling.

Is that Mrs. Coakley cooking bacon?
Is that John Pfister's wind that's breaking?
When we inhale, no smell's forsaken.
We can even smell a scalp that's flaking.

A week-old bagel, some cheap shampoo,
What pleasures us is lost on you.
With nostrils open at summer's dusk,
We can smell, from afar, a dachshund's musk.

ARTIE AND FRED
NEW YORK CITY

UNDERTOW

This is the pits.
I'm no Mark Spitz.
I prefer, on the whole,
My water safely in a bowl.

ARCHIE
LEVITTOWN, PENNSYLVANIA

PHILOSOPHICAL

Do I look like I've been caught
Deep in thought and with emotion fraught?
As if some distant land I've charted?
Don't be fooled. It's just that I've farted.

JASPER
ROWAYTON, CONNECTICUT

I LIKE TO BARK

I like to bark for no reason—
Don't need no mailman, don't need no rabbit.
I bark because it's deeply pleasin';
It goes much deeper than mere habit.

I'm happy to be one of those pets
Whose barking amounts to a kind of Tourette's.
Or, to put it more starkly,
I tend to see life through a glass barkly.

RUFUS
COLD SPRING, NEW YORK

JE NE SAIS QUOI

This stunning sense of style, it comes to me
As others' breathing does, effortlessly:
Kerchief of fetching sky-blue georgette,
Offset by a scarlet hood—a fashion minuet.

JAX
JACKSONVILLE, FLORIDA

HIDING

I'm hiding
I'm hiding from you
I'm hiding from the things I've
done

The naughty things
The thing on the couch
The thing on the rug
The thing on the basement floor.

And the things you'll never find.

BART
NEW YORK CITY

DREAMING OF BOOTY

When I'm tired of self-pity and pouting,
I daydream that I'm out on an outing.
Sometimes I like to pretend I'm a sailor
Who picks up a Doberman down on the dock,
Or a fiercely proud Clydesdale in Barbie's horse trailer.
I imagine I'm someone whom no one dares mock.

You see a Chihuahua, but in my own mind
I'm a burly Saint Bernard with a great big behind.

CHACHI
SPRINGFIELD, PENNSYLVANIA

THE TASTE OF ME

A smidgen of oak
A hint of cherry
A pinch of mint
And juniper berry.
What could that taste on my tongue really be?
Why, it's the fresh and fruity bouquet of me!

PENNY
DARIEN, CONNECTICUT

MY BIG BONE

Chew, chew, chew, chew
Lick, lick, lick, lick
Gnaw, gnaw, gnaw, gnaw

And so it goes
My big bone

MICKEY
TESUQUE, NEW MEXICO

PAW DITTY

I love my paws
Because.
Because they're so much more than feet
More than something soft and neat
To circumambulate the street.
They're gentle, but tough—not effete-y.
Everything about them's meaty.

When I lick my paws, I'm Warren Beatty,
The King of Haiti, the Real Slim Shady.
I regard my paws as a single deity.

When something gnaws at me,
It's my soothing paw that paws at me.
There ought to be laws with a special clause
Enforcing the protection of my paws
With gauze
From dust and dirt and hurt and harm.
No rabbit's feet have such charm.
Here's one of my favorite saws:

*You can't say nothing without
   due cause
To diss or deprecate my paws.*

*There are those that hems and
   those that haws,
But I'm not ambivalent about
   my paws.
So, honey, you can keep your feet—
Just give me paws when I meet the
   street.*

AMEE
STONE RIDGE, NEW YORK

WHAT'S YOU PROBLEM?

I knows why you starin',
I knows how you feels.
Where most doggies has legs
I got only wheels.

Is you chucklin' that I challenged?
Do the situation make you laugh?
Good. Come closer, and before
*   you knows it,*
My teeth be in your calf.

JAX
JACKSONVILLE, FLORIDA

BLISS

Nothing makes me happier that I belong to this species
Than the wind-wafted scent of another dog's feces.

LUNA
HELLERTOWN, PENNSYLVANIA

THROW THE DAMN BALL

Why do you abuse me?
You throw it, then confuse me.
It's tiresome the way you mimic a toss.
What's the point of pointing out who's boss?
Please don't tease me. Why do you stall?
Goddammit, you human—just throw the damn ball!

OSCAR
NEW YORK CITY

GROWL

I saw the best of my generation
barking madly moonward,
hysterical leather chew addicts on Harleys,
smelly and proud

MAX
GARDENA, CALIFORNIA

MUD

Lord, I crave mud,
Earth's own lovely crud.
Love is grand, but I choose
The grander grandeur of elemental ooze.

WILLIAM
GARDINER, NEW YORK

REQUIEM FOR THE NEW DOG

How dare you buy a terrier?
I thought that you'd be warier
Of making my life any hairier,
By putting up this barrier.

How would the missus feel
If you brought home a second
  spouse?
So get rid of Rover for real
Or get the hell out of my house.

DAISY
SOUTH DARTMOUTH,
MASSACHUSETTS

HERE'S AN IDEA

Just humping and humping—
It's beginning to bore the little lady and me some.
So may we suggest a friendly threesome?

SNACK AND SOFA
NEW YORK CITY

WHAT MAN IS THAT?

Who's that man in your bed?
Did you ask me if he could stay?
He smells like beets
And he touched your teats!
We had such a good thing going, it
Now appears you're blowing it.
If I had hands, I'd be throwing shit.

What's he got that I don't got?
Don't answer that. He's not that hot.
Are you aware he took my spot?
I honestly hope he throws a clot.
God forbid you ever tie the knot!

Please tell me it's a one-night stand
Or this stud will find himself unmanned.

SKIPPY
VERONA, NEW JERSEY

LIFE IS A
JOURNEY

Are we there yet?
Are we there yet?
Are we there yet?
Are we there yet?

Are we there yet?

COSBY
LUTHERVILLE, MARYLAND

WHAT WE
LEFT BEHIND

I love to lie in autumn leaves
And think of you and smile,
Remembering just where it was
We left our fragrant pile.

MILLHOUSE
CAMBRIDGE, MASSACHUSETTS

GRADUATION DAY

The tassel's
A hassle.
I feel like an assle.

ROVER
NEW YORK CITY

'TIS THE SEASON

'Tis the season
To be jolly.
That's what they sell us—
Oh, what folly!

Give me some quaaludes,
Xanax and rum,
Some naked elves,
And I'll show you some fun.

NINA
AGOURA HILLS, CALIFORNIA

EATING DISORDER

Half a can of wet food,
Half a cup of dry.
It never changes
And I'd like to know why.

FRED
CASTRO VALLEY, CALIFORNIA

TIRED OF ATTIRE

Surely you jest
To imagine I enjoy being this badly dressed.
Can you not see I feel ashamed and stressed?
Please, please give the clothes thing a rest.

ZOE
NEW YORK CITY

WHILE WATCHING DALMATIANS ON TV

Sure he's got a shinier coat,
But—excuuuse me—is that a reason to gloat?
And the way he lets her examine his jowls
Gives me a gut-wrenching
*   pain in my bowels.*
Why is he he and me me?
He still has to lift his hind
*   leg to pee.*

MILO
MOUNT VERNON, NEW YORK

POME IN ME

Punk chew ashun and spellunk R not, my game
but I, got; a pome in me all the same
in wich the fust 2 lines they shorely rime
but the nexx too dont even come close
I once seen the washintun momament on a car trip
man that wuz Sumpin

RORY
NEW YORK CITY

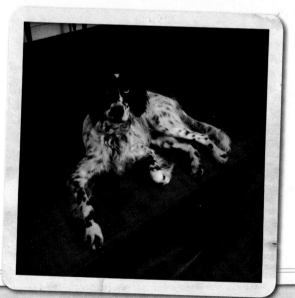

I STUNK

I stunk
From a skunk
So I stand in this gunk
To get rid of the funk.

But, mate, do me a favor
And enhance this flat flavor
With a splash of Ketel One
Or something equally fun.

Maybe a fifth of Stolichnaya
'Cause I'd like to get higha.

ZERO
RIVERDALE, NEW YORK

CROSSING OVER

Lately, I've found myself confessing
More and more that I love cross-dressing.
I may be a moth, a butterfly, or bee—
Any old drag makes this hag feel free.
A hornet? A mosquito? Dame Edna? A tick?
As long as it's gaudy and bawdy, it does the trick.

NELL
LAWRENCEVILLE, GEORGIA

STICK

Stick.
Mysterious and woody.
How I love thee.
So loyal and true.
Why do I crave you so?
Never would I let you go.

Hark!
What's that lying in yonder trees?
Another stick?

Stick.
Mysterious and woody.
How I love thee. . . .

SPROCKET
KIRKWOOD, NEW YORK

MY BOWL RUNNETH OVER

Sticky, licky, icky, chunky
Funky mound of indescribable sustenance.
Crusty, musty serving of lumpy mass.
I am the luckiest dog in the world.

AMEE
STONE RIDGE, NEW YORK

SLACK

It's true, you know, what they say:
We really like to be in a pack.
But not leashed to a human who
*   walks us for pay.*
Would someone please cut us
*   some slack?*
We'd like to have our freedom
*   back.*

PHOEBE, CHLOE, AND RIPLEY
PROVIDENCE, RHODE ISLAND

COLD COMFORT

Can you spare a hug
For a frosty pug?

CURLY
BABYLON, NEW YORK

UNCONDITIONAL

Here's how you can tell that I love you much more
Than your ungrateful children or hectoring wife:
When you walk, as you do every night, through the door,
It's the happiest moment of this doggie's life.

CASSIDY
LONG BEACH, NEW YORK

GIVE IT TO ME

Give it to me, give it to me,
Give it to me now,
Give me that dog treat,
Give me that little bone-shaped
   treat.
Put it right here in my kisser.
Drop the baked good, you miserable
   pisser!
What did I ever do to you, you
   freakin' moron
To deserve your cruel games and hateful teasing?
Just give me the friggin' cookie!

CLIFF
NEWHALL, IOWA

WHO'S THAT
TASTY MORSEL?

Who's that tasty morsel in the park?
Your little white feet.
Your tiny firm body.
Your perky ears.
I want you in my mouth.

NEKO
WASHINGTON, D.C.

THE LOVE SONG OF J. EMMA PRUFROCK

I don't drop my trou
For just any bowwow.
I don't like impatient dogs and I don't like crude.
I'm a delicate lady and I like to be wooed.
I don't like Don Juans and I don't like scenes.
Otherwise, feel free to get into my jeans.

EMMA
OCEANSIDE, NEW YORK

I LOVE YOU, JUST NOT THAT MUCH

I love you, just not that much.
It's why I recoil from your awkward touch.
Are you aware of your meddling insistence?
Could you please adore me from a distance?

LUCY
HIGHLAND PARK, ILLINOIS

I THINK THAT I SHALL NEVER SEE

I think that I shall never see
A poem as lovely as a half-eaten
  sandwich
That's been on the sidewalk for hours,
Absorbing a rainbow of footwear odors,
Traces of dried spittle, and soupçon of
  week-old urine.
There is nothing to compare to the
  soiled remains
Of a Genoa-salami-and-swiss that
  contains multitudes,
In whose every bite I can sample the
  city and taste life once again.

JACKIE
BROOKLYN, NEW YORK

SMELL, DON'T TELL

When I smell you
I don't tell you.
Why hurt your pride
Just because you smell like
 something that died?

I work hard to fight the feeling
 Of distaste when you send me
  reeling.
 But why should I your cheery
  mood deflate

Just because I'm bowled over by what you ate?
I'd tell you what your dinner was,
But what's the point of killing your buzz?

QUINCY DOODLE
FISHKILL, NEW YORK

IDENTITY CRISIS

Perhaps I'm a sqrat—
Part rodent, part squirrel.
Or perhaps a girzelle—
Part gazelle and part girl.
My self-esteem's shaky, my
*   ancestry a muddle;*
Perhaps I'm just the dog you're
*   least likely to cuddle.*

PUNKY
RICE LAKE, WISCONSIN

HAMBURGER HELPLESS

Excuse me! This burger is rubber,
*   not meat.*
If I were your owner, you'd be out
*   on the street.*
I'm really, truly, at a loss.
That you'd think that I'd think that
*   this has special sauce.*
So take this offending facsimile back
Unless you want to see a Big Dog
*   Attack.*

ROVER
NEW YORK CITY

RHYMING IS FOR CATS

Rhyming is for cats,
with their tiny, tiny lips
and pretentious little way of nibbling their food.
When you drop them,
they always land on their feet,
which is tedious, like knowing that at the end of the line
you're always going to get a rhyme.
You want your poem to rhyme?
I have one word for you:
Pussy.

SOMA
CHICAGO

THE LIFE I LEAD

What life is this,
The life I lead?
What do I want?
What do I need?

What's my journey?
What's my quest?
Am I doomed?
Am I blessed?

Or am I destined
To be a loner—
Content to lie here
With my boner?

RUFUS

COLD SPRING, NEW YORK

NEXT TIME

Next time you'll think twice before you go away
After I've asked you to sit! And stay!

NIKKI
KREAMER, PENNSYLVANIA

ONE FOR THE ROAD

Alone with my thoughts, here joined by spirits
Seen and unseen, unblended and neat—
No more an ugly pug, but a noble besotted knight,
Purebred, alone, neutered and knackered.

SNACK
NEW YORK CITY

SLOUCHING TO NOWHERE

Turning and turning in a ridiculous circle,
I cannot hear myself think.
Not that my thoughts are all that
  interesting.
Mostly I think about why I keep turning
And turning in a stupid circle,
And all I can come up with is the fear
That things will fall apart if I stop.
Isn't that crazy?

GRIZABELLA
SARANAC LAKE, NEW YORK

THE LITTLE BASTARDS

Last month it was worms,
Last week it was ticks,
And today I have fleas.
Always soaking in chemicals
And sprinkled with powders.
I want to run and play with the other dogs.
So kill the little bastards already!

ABE
NEW YORK CITY

HERE, NOW

Away from the sniffing & digging
& chasing & chewing
on heavenly deck
I find a moment
called the present

TACO
MERCED, CALIFORNIA

NOT A CHANCE

"Here!" "Here!" "Come Here!" "Here!"
All day long you assault my ear.
Do you really think the command's unclear?
And when I don't move, you look so austere!
Hey, I don't mean to be
*   cavalier,*
But why don't you just go
*   have a beer,*
With a human being who's
*   more your peer?*
'Cause my ass has no
*   intention of getting in gear*
And coming any closer to
*   there than right here.*

LENA
PRATTSVILLE, NEW YORK

I WISH I WERE A RABBIT

I wish I were a rabbit,
Hopping to and fro.
I wish I were a rabbit,
Not an eagle, not a doe.

For if I were a rabbit,
Soft and snowy white,
I'd be getting laid,
Every day and every night.

BRUTUS
CORAL SPRINGS, FLORIDA

RRRRRUUUUHHH!

Ruh ruh!
Rrrrrrrrrrrrrrr....
Rruuumff!
Rrrrrrrr....
Rufff-a.
Rufff-a.
Ruh!

L'IL ABNER
NEW YORK CITY

MY SOUL IS FRISKY

My soul is frisky,
Held captive by my youth,
In innocence prone
To do the uncouth.

I'm sorry I shat on the carpet.

SHEA
NEW YORK CITY

BRING YOUR
FACE CLOSER

Lick, lick, lick.
It's what I do.
Lick is what I'd like
To do to you.

COSBY
LUTHERVILLE, MARYLAND

ODE TO ERRANDS

O, how superb
To pull away from the curb.
Never more alive
Than when we hit sixty-five,
With the wind in our hair
And our snouts splitting the air.

BARKY AND NANCY
DRIPPING SPRINGS, TEXAS

WHY BOTHER?

Why bother?
You must think I'm pretty dumb,
That all you can say to me is "Come."
What about your husband's affair
With your son's therapist?
His jacket's covered with her hair.
That's just one thing you've
     completely missed.

Did you think your migraines weren't mental,
But biological? Incidental?
And whether or not Brad's got ADD,
That description fits you to a T.
Eleven years to choose a couch?
And you call Jeremy a slouch?
And this has nothing to do with your domineering father?
Honestly.
Why bother?

TUCKER
FAIRFIELD, CONNECTICUT

YOU ASKED WHY I TWITCH

Which twitch are you talking about?
The twitch as I evade some airborne cat
In my leashless Chagall dreams?
Or the twitch I twitch if there's a glitch
In my fantasy of winning Best in Show?
Or is it the twitch I twitch as the pitch
I pitch in some canine All-Star game
Is lined back at my snout
And I know in a second I'll be knocked
  out?

MICKEY
TESUQUE, NEW MEXICO

WHAT A DOG WANTS

Don't kiss me on the lips. It's a sin,
Because I have no way of knowing
Where those lips have been.

KINA
NEW PALTZ, NEW YORK

KEEPSAKE'S END

Your mother's mother's afghan, treasure from the past,
Each stitch a loving message to future family cast.
Until just now the scent was faint, of sandalwood and rose,
But my incontinence has brought its fragrant journey to a close.

RUFUS
COLD SPRING, NEW YORK

THE DOG I WAS

There was nothing I wouldn't chase,
Including my tail. Life was a race
To get from smell to smell and place to place.

No woods too dense, no bluff too steep—
I had miles to run, then ran in my sleep.
I needed no hint to sprint
*   through snowdrifts deep.*

The point was always to
*   leave all behind.*
But the years were in the
*   end unkind*
And by speed and need I was
*   no longer defined.*
Now I'm free at last to run in
*   your mind.*

WILLOW
WABAN, MASSACHUSETTS

112

IS YOUR PET SPECIAL ENOUGH?

We are looking for photographs of dogs and cats for possible inclusion in future publications by the authors. If you would like your unique pet to be considered for literary immortality, send us your high-quality digital photographs (no human in the shot, please!) along with the following information to **photos@catanddogphotos.com**:

Pet's name and breed, owner's name, address, phone number, and e-mail address.

You represent that you are the sole owner of the rights granted herein, including copyright, and that you have read and agreed to the following terms of submission: By sending us your photos, you acknowledge that they become the nonexclusive property of the authors (R. D. Rosen, Harry Prichett, and Rob Battles) and the authors' licensees and assigns, who will have the right, without further notice or consideration, to reproduce and use them in future books, calendars, and other publications in any media, throughout the world, in all languages, and in related advertising and promotion.

Thank you!

ACKNOWLEDGMENTS

The authors would like to thank all the owners of these remarkably literate dogs for allowing us to give their animals' poems a wider audience. We are indebted to our agent, Victoria Skurnick, of the Levine Greenberg Literary Agency, and our editor, Philip Budnick, of Plume, for seeing the value of these poems, despite the frequency with which the word *bowels* shows up in them. Extra treats go to Clare Ferraro, Kathryn Court, Leigh Butler, Sabila Khan, Ashley Pattison McClay, Matthew Daddona, Norina Frabotta, Lavina Lee, Daniel Lagin, Jaya Miceli, Lucia Kim, Elizabeth Keenan, John Fagan, and Norman Lidofsky, of Penguin Group (USA), for their roles in publishing this collection. Our gratitude also goes to Joyce Friedman, without whose contributions this book would have both a little less bark and a little less bite.

ABOUT THE AUTHORS

R. D. ROSEN is an Edgar Award–winning mystery novelist and the author of several nonfiction books, including *A Buffalo in the House* and the forthcoming *Such Good Girls*, the story of the Holocaust's hidden child survivors. He once studied poetry with Robert Lowell and Elizabeth Bishop. Read more about him at rdrosen.com.

HARRY PRICHETT has written and performed for the improv comedy groups Chicago City Limits and Radio Active Theater, is the creator of the off-off-Broadway one-man show *Work=Pain=Success*, and has appeared on television and in film. He has collaborated with R. D. Rosen on comedy segments for National Public Radio's *All Things Considered*. Read more at harryprichett.com.

ROB BATTLES works in the entertainment business for an inordinately successful content company, and has made it his business over the years to encourage people to consume as much media as possible. He has written and produced for public radio stations and NPR, and has relied on humor to avoid beatings since the third grade.

Together, Rosen, Prichett, and Battles cowrote the *New York Times* best sellers *Bad Cat*, *Bad Dog*, and *Bad President*.